Making the Playground:
a Key Stage 2 project in Design Technology, Art, English and Mathematics

Making the Playground:
a Key Stage 2 project in Design Technology, Art, English and Mathematics

Eileen Adams

𝑡𝑏

Trentham Books

First published in 1993 by Trentham Books Limited

Trentham Books Limited
Westview House
734 London Road
Oakhill
Stoke-on-Trent
England ST4 5NP

British Library Cataloguing in publication Data
A catalogue record of this book is available at the British Library

ISBN: 0 948080 92 2

ACKNOWLEDGEMENTS

Eileen Adams
front cover
back cover
pages 5, 10, 18, 22, 27, 29, 31, 37

David Stone
22, 23, 25, 33, 37.

Commercial Signs
24

Designed and typeset by Trentham Print Design Limited, Chester
and printed by Bemrose Shafron Limited, Chester.

CONTENTS

Introduction

In 1991, an evaluation study was commissioned by Gillespie School and funded by Islington Education Authority to document the work done by Class 3 (Y4) with the Islington Schools Environmental Project (ISEP) on the design of markings for the school playground. The evaluation was a group effort, led by Eileen Adams, aiming to provide feedback for those involved and to enable them to share their experience with others. This book is based on their report.

I have re-established my belief in the importance of good planning. We have also explored how such projects can relate to the attainment targets for the National Curriculum. I am learning more about what is appropriate for different age groups and what are reasonable expectations. I can see it will be necessary to do more work and evaluation to compare projects and determine why particular processes work or do not work with particular age groups.

The evaluation has given us an opportunity to reflect on our ideas and our work. It has enabled us to structure our experience, which has perhaps given us a different view of our work and has given it a different meaning. It has reinforced our conviction that what we have done has been valuable, but it has obliged us to question certain aspects of our work. It has made me realise that although a number of people can share the same experience, they will all have very different perceptions of it. David Stone.

There are three aspects of the project which are relevant to other schools: a focus on environmental design studies; environmental improvements; and working with an outside agency. Particularly important, the work relates closely to the requirements of the new Orders for Design and Technology in the National Curriculum at key stage 2. It satisfies the attainment targets and shows how environmental design projects can be incorporated in programmes of studies in primary schools. It concentrates on the environment, but also incorporates the notion of games and play as systems and gives some consideration to artefacts which can be used in play activities. It is not always possible for pupils to realise their ideas in environmental design projects, but here, with the co-operation of a community arts group and the PTA, their proposals were realised and they saw the results for themselves. This book describes the experiences of those involved at Gillespie School and gives advice to others contemplating similar projects.

Background

☐ Gillespie Primary School

Gillespie School in Islington, North London, is a primary school of some 200 pupils. Built in 1878, it is an imposing three story brick building, surrounded by tarmac playgrounds, standing in a street of terraced housing close to the Arsenal Football Ground. The school has a tradition of inviting outsiders to work with the pupils and teachers. Janet Eccles, the teacher of Class 3 (Y4), had worked at the school for six years. She welcomed the playground project as an opportunity for collaborative learning.

☐ ISEP

ISEP is an environmental Arts and Education team which works with schools, offering curriculum support to create opportunities for pupils and teachers to engage in design projects. A key idea underlying the work is to enable people to have an opportunity to shape their environment and improve environmental quality. There is generally a physical outcome to the design work. ISEP's main purpose is to develop environmental arts, to determine how the arts can contribute to our lives. The emphasis is on practical projects. There is also a commitment to equal opportunities, particularly in relation to children's play. David Stone, the Director of ISEP, is a qualified teacher employed by Islington Education Authority to offer support for schools to realise Islington's Environmental Education policy.

☐ Background to Project

The playground markings project was initiated by a concern to improve opportunities for play. The staff and play supervisors discussed the use of the playground and the fact that the previous markings were not being used. In the past, they had been a popular focus for play activities, especially for the younger pupils. Now they had faded, and were ignored by the children. The initial proposal was to reinstate the original markings and perhaps to extend them to other areas of the playground. ISEP was invited to work with the teachers and pupils to help them determine what was needed and to find a way to implement their ideas. The Friends of Gillespie agreed to meet the cost of having the new markings painted.

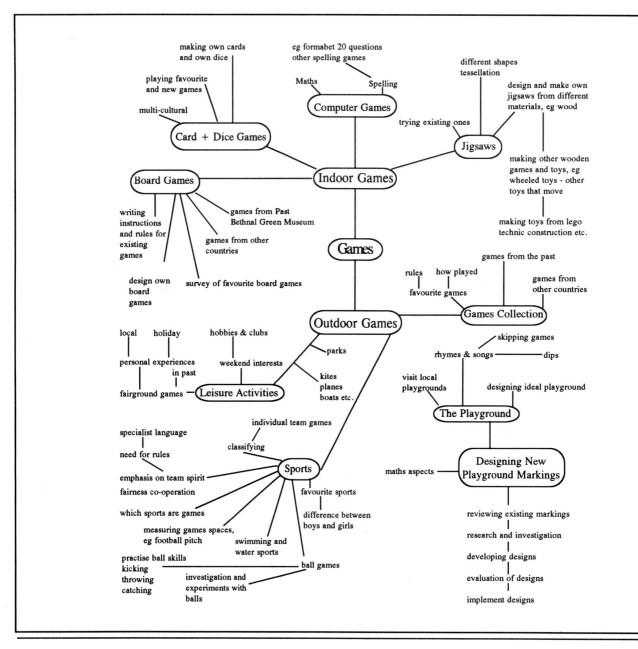

Planning: topic on games

Janet Eccles, the teacher of Class 3 (year 4, second year juniors) worked with David Stone (ISEP) to prepare an outline course. The teacher planned a cross-curricular programme of work for the spring term on the topic of games. This included consideration of sports, leisure activities, indoor games, computer games, ball games and work on bullying. These studies provided a context for the work on playground markings, for which David Stone did the detailed planning. They provided a background and a springboard for the design studies and helped the children think more fully about the purpose of their design activity. Although the original plan provided a useful framework, some modifications were inevitably necessary, because of the weather or because the timing did not work out as anticipated. David Stone was able to work with the class for eight Thursday mornings plus time for preparation and follow-up.

TEACHER: *I was a bit worried that I would not be up to it. I was a bit daunted at first, but excited at the same time. I hoped that it would bring the class together as a group. I thought of Technology as making things, using construction toys, modelling with junk materials and woodwork. I had thought of design as a 3D activity, which involved constructing and making things. David Stone emphasised the idea of space and manipulating a visual language.*

ISEP: *There is always a fear coming into new situations and the worry —will we be able to bring it off? I prepared an outline programme and the teacher filled out the project to cover a wider range of educational objectives. We hoped to develop cross-curricular work. Other projects I had done were more design-specific. I took more trouble to plan this one and to accommodate the requirements of the National Curriculum. This made me focus more specifically on the range of learning activities involved. The implication here is that there needs to be more time created for planning programmes of work and training teachers to handle it.*

HEAD TEACHER: *The project started with an awareness that the group identity of this particular class was not strong. The teacher identified working together as a difficulty. At the same time, we wanted to improve the playground environment to extend the range of uses. In the playground markings project, we brought the two ideas together.*

☐ English

Each child will write about their favourite outdoor game, how it is played and what the rules are. This will lead to examining the popularity of various games, the differences between the preferences of boys and girls of different ages, and will result in an illustrated book of games to play.

- Children will be expected to participate as speakers and listeners in class discussion.

- They will be encouraged to read different types of books related to the topic, to seek information, ideas and develop an understanding of the concept of 'games': eg: plans, explanations, descriptions, rules, stories.

- They will be expected to record the results of their investigations to include: interviews, instructions, creative writing, poetry.

- Additional exercises will include spelling and a weekly group handwriting session.

☐ History: Games from the Past

- We will find out about games children used to play, try playing or making them and find the similarities or differences between Victorian games and those played today (eg: top spinning, hoops, cup and ball, hopscotch).

- Visit to Bethnal Green Museum to investigate games.

- Interview parents and grandparents.

☐ Geography: Games from Other Countries

- We will discover games children play abroad, try playing them and find the similarities and differences between them and those we play in the UK (eg: marbles, throwing up nuts, kites).

ref: Topic Pack *Games Around the World*, Junior Education *Play Without Frontiers*, Bright Ideas Teachers Handbook *Language Resources*.

- Investigate games played abroad — possible visit to Museum of Mankind.

☐ Music: Rhymes and Songs

- We will make a collection of favourite rhymes, songs and dips and add any new rhymes we discover from other countries or the past (ref: books and people).

- We will try out skipping rhymes and those connected with ball games.

- Perhaps we might invent some new rhymes.
  ref: Bright Ideas *Language Resources*, Oink and Pearl Skipping, Music Time.

☐ Dance

- We will be working with Jane from the White Lion Centre on the theme of playground games.

☐ Maths

- Pupils will be expected to extract, collect, analyse information.

- Pupils will be expected to select materials to use for a task and to make and test predictions when investigating and making games.

- Pupils will develop an understanding of number and number operations when playing number games.

- Pupils will develop an understanding of length and measurement eg: measuring playground area; making scale plans.

- Pupils will develop an understanding of analogue and digital time.

- Pupils will develop an understanding of shape: eg: using shapes to make playground games, jigsaws and designs.

☐ Science

- Pupils will be encouraged to formulate hypotheses; interpret data and record findings of experiments — eg: bar charts.

- Pupils will create simple databases to store information on playground games. Pupils will make a study of materials — describe attributes, sequencing, and group materials by characteristics.

- Pupils will study the nature of forces — push/pull can make things move; describe how a simple toy uses mechanisms.

☐ Art, Design Technology

- Recording and analysing playground space.

- Designing new playground markings and visualising changes.

- Designing and making board games, toys.

☐ PE

- Ball skills; dance; swimming.

☐ RE

- Chinese New Year

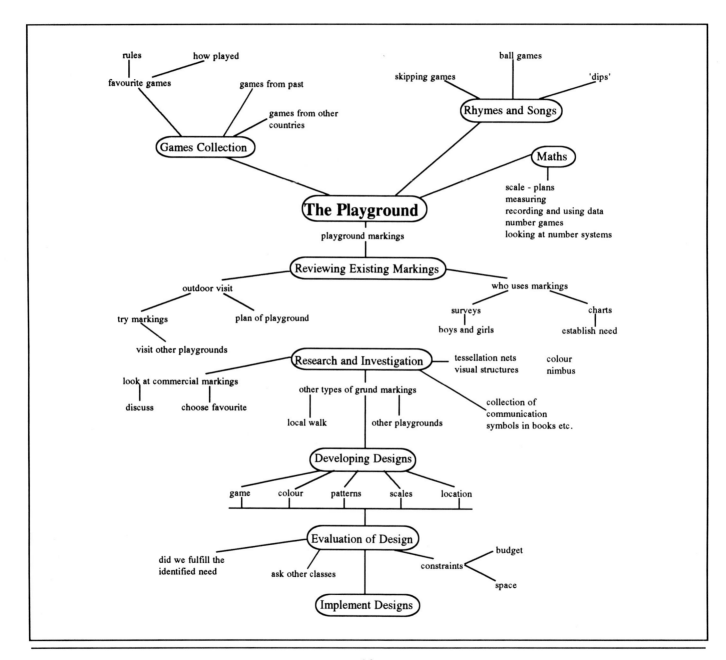

Planning:
Playground Markings project

☐ Aims and Objectives

- To stimulate an interest in numbers and signs and develop language skills.

- To develop awareness and knowledge of the environment.

- To encourage co-operation, good self-esteem, group pride and multicultural appreciation.

- To develop an appreciation of design processes and design skills.

☐ Activities

1 Assessing and Defining Human Needs

- Introduction: slide presentation of previous work by ISEP at the school.

- Environmental awareness exercise.

- Visit another playground to try out some of the markings (weather permitting).

- Make a scale plan of the playground, mark on the plan existing markings.

- Surveys, interviews on use of playground. Bar charts.

- Establish need for change.

2 Research and Investigation

- Study of symbols and commercial markings, discuss, choose favourites.

- Street work to find what other types of markings are possible. Recording information. Study of markings — eg visit to Ambler School.

- Exploration of games — class to bring in examples. What games do we know?

- Can we invent any? What games are played around the world? Study of structures, tessellation nets, colour.

3 Developing Designs

- Consider possibilities for developing new markings to stimulate games in playground. Take into account: games, colour, pattern, scale, location.

4 Evaluation of Design

- Did we fulfil the identified needs? Consult other classes.

- Choosing which design to use — consider constraints, budget, space.

5 Implementation

- Arrange for markings to be painted. Class to monitor use of markings.

- Record the project. Prepare display and assembly.

Work in progress

☐ Games

The teacher introduced a study of games, including consideration of play activities and the different games played in the playground. The class produced written work describing and explaining games. Art work provided an opportunity for pupils to explore ideas about their ideal playground. The idea of play was a theme which underpinned their studies throughout the term. Working with the White Lion Centre on Tuesdays, the class explored in greater depth different kinds of play activities based on balls. For instance, gender issues, such as girls playing football, were discussed. The idea of rules determining behaviour was considered. Different ball games were played. The class discussed, wrote about and explored through their art work the experience of bullying and how to deal with it. This work informed, extended and enriched the work done specifically within the design project.

☐ Introduction to Playground Project

David Stone from ISEP presented a slide show to explain how a previous project at Gillespie School had developed play structures for the playground. The key message was that children can change their environment. Discussion following the slide show encouraged the children to share their perceptions of the playground and their experience of play there.

ISEP: *The introduction consisted of twenty slides of previous environmental projects at the school. It lasted about half an hour which was probably ten minutes too long. My main aim was to show the pupils that the work they will do will lead to tangible outcomes. Past projects were used as evidence of this. The slides showed some obscure details of parts of the playground and this led to discussion about exact locations. This suggested the idea of an environmental awareness game which we used in the second session.*

☐ Environment Familiarisation

Pupils were shown photographs of details from the playground to encourage them to observe more carefully and look again at a familiar environment.

TEACHER: *The children had to find six places in the school playground, which they identified from details on photographs. It built on their curiosity and was used as a focusing device to develop environmental awareness and observational skills. It also developed verbal skills in describing and explaining their experience.*

☐ Survey

The children worked in pairs to find out how the playground is currently used. They wanted to know who uses the markings. They designed survey sheets to record information collected from interviews with pupils in other classes. The children prepared charts to show the different games favoured by boys and girls, which gave them experience of tallying and tabulating information.

> TEACHER: *The survey was a good idea for social interaction, when pupils had to work together in pairs to plan their questionnaire and recording sheet. They had to record, interpret and present data.*

☐ Plan Making

The class was divided into four groups and each group asked to measure a part of the playground, using trundle wheels.

> ISEP: *The whole group was introduced to the idea of plan making and explored concepts of measurement, distance, direction, angles and symbols. The class are energetic, but once they understand a task they tend to meet it with much enthusiasm. They particularly appear to enjoy locating the photographs, a theme developed from last week, although they seemed equally keen on using the trundle wheels. All apparently had a good understanding of a plan view and were very competent with the measuring and recording, due to previous input by their class teacher.*

Scale Plan

One group of pupils prepared a scale plan, using the information provided by all the groups. This brought into play measurement, scale, the use of a key and a colour code.

ISEP: *A group of four pupils were chosen to work intensively all morning to turn our measurements into a scale plan. They were chosen from the top maths group as it was felt they would benefit most from this complex task. The group were given an explanation of scale, how it works and why we need to make plans. Using the simple scale of 1:100 and a T square, the group successfully drew their plan.*

TEACHER: *Working on the scale plan was useful. Different groups measured different parts of the playground, then they put all their information onto one plan which had to be drawn to scale. This was to be used as the basis for our design work, so there was a real purpose for maths activities.*

Study of Signs

A study of signs and symbols helped the children explore the notion that ideas can be communicated visually. They looked at a number of signs and symbols from different sources such as traffic signs, symbols used at airports, directional signs and discussed how they communicated particular ideas. A quiz based on these added excitement to the exercise.

Study of Markings and Play Area

A study of catalogues of commercially produced markings provided opportunities for critical appraisal. The aim here was to develop vocabulary and criteria to help the children identify quality.

A visit to Ambler School enabled the children to study play structures and markings at first hand in an unfamiliar environment and to be more objective about their judgements.

ISEP: *Tried out markings and made drawings at Ambler School. Back at school we continued with design work and writing rules for games......next week, I will suggest to class we prototype the circle design (cat and mouse) and the ivy maze, because it brings lots of ideas together. Work on A3 paper.*

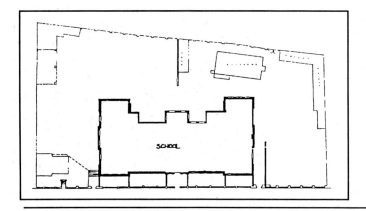

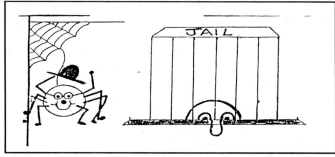

☐ Generating and Developing Ideas for Change

The class worked in four groups, each with a different theme suggested by the adults: maze, rings, leaves, while the fourth considered where to place the new markings in the playground. The groups played design games and tried brainstorming to generate ideas. Following that, each pupil worked individually to develop their own idea. The children had to write an explanation of how their game should be played and to explain it to the group. Each group was asked to choose the best idea from their group, then to work co-operatively on its development. Designs were drawn up for three markings. Groups used different techniques to develop their ideas, such as tessellation games using metal washers and a cardboard maze; computers using the SMILE disc; or a collection of leaves, which could be moved around to create various shapes.

☐ Evaluation of Ideas

It was necessary to test out the ideas. This was done through the class comparing the different possibilities and discussing the positioning of the markings on the playground. One group tried to visualise the impact of the designs on the playground space. The class also tested out their ideas in discussion with Rita Butterfield, a play supervisor, who advised them on safety considerations and commented on the their work.

ISEP: *A group of five children talked to the groups who produced the designs and drew these on our map of the playground. We then visited the playground to see if the ground was level and if we had enough space. This resulted*

Game	Maze	Tree of Life	Colour Circles
Resources	Smile programme Tiles tessellation game	Leaves, Books on Trees	Cirles and Tiles
Activity	Design a maze with a beginning and an end.	Identify leaves, draw trees, rubbings from leaves.	Explore symmetry and pattern making.
Evalnation	With hard copy test maze	Test game with another member of the class.	Test game with class.

in changes to the children's original ideas. Rita Butterfield, a helper, then visited the class and looked at the designs and gave her ideas. This led to further changes and informed our final decision on the layout. It was interesting to note that the question game was first located in a small corner near the ball games area where the designer regularly plays. Mrs. Butterfield picked up on the fact that this game required a quiet space and the other two a run-around space. Her input was invaluable.

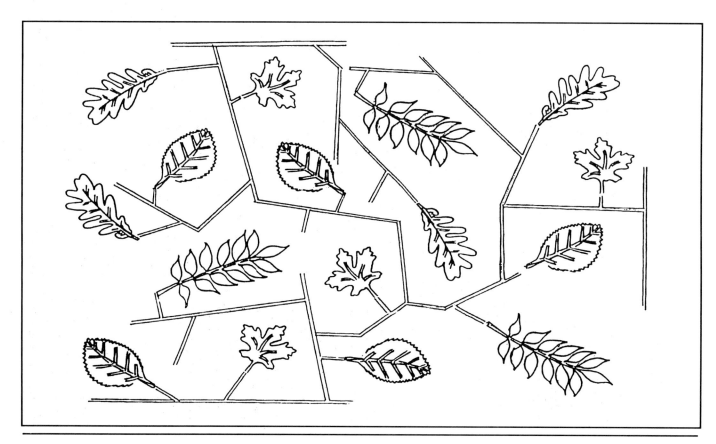

Implementation

Final designs were drawn up by David Stone from the children's work for the painters to use as a guide. The children's ideas were not significantly altered, except to simplify the designs to make them more suitable for painting. Lynne, Bill and Alan from Comprehensive Signs translated the pupils' designs into markings on the playground. Lynne's advice was that there is a need for pupils to undertake an appraisal of the playground before contemplating any changes. This should include the physical state of the playground and the condition of the tarmac surface. It needs to include a study of existing movement patterns within the space. During the design phase, careful thought should be given to the positioning of the markings and to the size of the individual areas to be painted, so that the markings do not cause safety problems or conflict with other uses of the space. The design should avoid cracks and drains. Large areas of colour can wear badly, depending on the amount of traffic, weather conditions and exposure to heat, cold, rain and air pollution. It is probably better to create a linear design with patches of colour, as this is likely to look better for longer. Colours such as white and yellow have greater impact than red or blue. It should be remembered that painted markings are not permanent, but probably have a life span of between two and five years.

It is a good idea to consult the firm who will paint the markings at the beginning of the design phase. Their contribution to the thinking can prove invaluable, as they are well aware of the practical considerations and constraints on the final design. They are also knowledgeable about the difficulties of painting the markings — the need for a clean surface in good condition; the problems of reading and interpreting other people's plans and designs; the need to translate the ideas into a larger scale; the activity of marking out the design in chalk and painting without mishap. The team used simple equipment such as a track marker and T square to help them draw parallel lines and had made full-size cardboard templates of the more complicated shapes in their workshop to save time and effort on site. The pupils witnessed the markings being chalked out, then tested them to check that they worked, discussing the practicalities with the painters. The markings were painted in the summer of 1991. Pupils are now monitoring how they are used.

THE TEACHER'S VIEW

☐ Personal and Social Development

The project was concerned with the development of social skills, encouraging children to work together in groups, recognising each other's strengths, valuing each other's work, valuing their own work, recognising that they were able to make a contribution, to see that parts were important to the whole. They were able to recognise needs —not just their own but those of other people. They developed skills in independent and collaborative working and many of them became less reliant on me as the teacher. They understood more about independence and inter-dependence. They became more responsible for their own work. The key thing was that we were working with a purpose.

☐ Roles

It has been a partnership between David and myself. I became more confident as we worked through. I set time limits on various activities, organised the groups and the class as a whole. I identified the educational needs. I created opportunities for appropriate learning activities. I had to consider the practicalities involved and to ensure continuity in the learning process. I had special knowledge of the pupils, what they had done before and what their capabilities were. I knew what demands we could make on the children. I was aware of the links across the curriculum. I needed to extend the work we did with David. Sometimes, I had to act as interpreter, so that the children would really understand what had been said or what they were expected to do. I helped identify appropriate resources such as books on games and picture references. I had to make sure that the children could distinguish between fantasy and reality. The teacher has to set a secure framework. There is a need to ensure appropriate social behaviour and to make sure the children work properly.

☐ Design Education

It gave the children a good grounding in design work — in planning, developing and evaluating ideas —a process they can apply to any kind of design work. There has been an emphasis on visual language. I anticipate that the pupils will be more capable in Technology. I think it is important to work from children's experience. Children can teach adults. It is important that we understand more of the culture of childhood and value a wider range of activities as a basis for learning experience.

ISEP's view

☐ Design Education

The project had both educational and design objectives. The use of playground markings as a focus for the work offered enormous potential to improve environmental quality and offer a context for a learning process. The time scale of a half day per week for a term worked well for the pupils. Logical and sequential work can be done like this. In the design phase of the work, it would probably have been better to work in a more concentrated way. This is necessary for creative work.

I can now see that not enough time was given to the design work, especially to testing out the designs. It would have been much better if we could have marked them out full size, even if this had been done with masking tape or chalk in the assembly hall, so that we had a large-scale mock up for the children to be able to test them properly. There was the time constraint which we imposed on ourselves to finish the work by the end of term. Children need to understand the constraints, such as the budget. Knowledge of the constraints imposed will influence their thinking about the design.

☐ Educational Benefits

As for educational benefits, the major one is an improved understanding of the design process by both the pupils and the teacher. I could see how their understanding of decision-making developed. Then there was critical thinking, especially about visual matters — how signs work, for instance. They understand better the language involved. As the project progressed, they seemed to be able to work better in teams, responding to each other, giving each other time and attention. Before the project, boys and girls would not work together. The children now have some understanding of the sequence of events involved in design in the real world; they are aware of the need to plan ahead, of the importance of working in a sequential and systematic way.

☐ Roles

My role has been to provide a structure for the work. The specific contribution I made was perhaps in developing visual awareness, promoting specific design skills, sequencing the work and identifying various thinking and creative processes. Any visitor provides stimulus and motivation for the children. There can be problems, just as there are when more than one adult works with a group of children. The pupils can try to play off one against the other. It is important for outsiders to work within the system already in place in the school and the particular classroom. They need to have an understanding of the pupil/teacher relationship which has already been established. The adults need to support each other and reinforce each other's work. This project offered a model for teachers to work with people from outside the school.

☐ Links

I created a link between the school and the community, connecting the children's work with the 'real' world. I also provided continuity between work that had gone on before in the school and the children's own work. I offered specific skills in terms of environmental familiarisation and design. It was an easy working relationship and very successful. You have to develop trust through working together. There is a problem in linking educational concerns with the outside world of commerce and bureaucracy. Companies will need educating to involve themselves more usefully in the development of the work, rather than be merely contractors, painting the designs. Local authorities will also need to be encouraged to adopt a different stance in relation to playground markings. Their view is currently based on the requirements of physical education and the markings they approve are either based on games courts and pitches or focused on numbers, counting, containment and control. The imagery of the commercial markings they recommend emphasises spiders trapped in webs, people in jail. Children's games are organic. Commercial and officially approved markings are static and limited.

☐ Environmental Improvement

Hopefully, there will be environmental benefits in terms of improvements to the playground and the creation of better opportunities for play. There will be tangible end products, which will affect the quality of playtime and the way children are able to play together and resolve conflicts. The design work has certainly given the girls more of a chance to have a say. Perhaps the markings will make girls' games more visible. Often playground markings, intended for physical education, emphasise ball games — and the playground ends up merely as a football pitch at playtime.

Pupils' perceptions

☐ Design

Everyone did a design, which had to be suitable for all ages and we had to think of safety. Some of the games were imaginative but impractical, such as those where you had to have trap doors, electrical wires, guns or a snake pit. But then you could always make it into a picture, so that it stood for the real thing. You had to think about safety, so that children would not bump into each other on the markings. You have to think where you are going to put the markings. They are a good idea as they give you more choice for play and they make the place look more lively. In design, you have to think of something from your mind, then draw it. It does not have to be neat, you just have to get the basic idea. It is helpful if you want to build a structure or make something, as you can think ahead, plan it.

☐ Group Work

When you worked in groups, you had to work on ideas together, to explain them to other people and hope they would like your idea. In teamwork, everybody works together, so somebody has half an idea that the others can extend. It is like thinking out loud. It is good to work in groups because you get more ideas. It is easier because everyone helps each other. You encourage each other. You have more manpower. Working alone, you are independent, you do what you like, you don't ask anyone else. You don't have to explain to anyone else. In a group, you have to think, to share ideas and learn not to open your mouth at the wrong time. In group work you can get a lot done quicker. On your own, you can't think of it. There can be problems. Sometimes you leave people out. Sometimes people interrupt all the time. You have to take turns. Sometimes people are stupid.

☐ Play

The playground is fun as there are lots of things to do. Children need fresh air and exercise for their health. Play helps you develop interests and prevents boredom, stops you getting into trouble. Play is good for exercise, and fresh air. You need a change from class work. After working, the brain needs a rest to do work afterwards. It is fun. You can meet with your friends. Children will have fun on the markings. Some of the ideas were quite dangerous. You need time to develop the ideas to improve the playground. You need to create opportunities for play and encourage children to be more active. Everything helps — the structures, the bench, the tyres — and of course, the markings.

The Supervisor's view

□ Play Environment

There are a range of structures which encourage different types of play. The structures help to develop a sense of security and confidence. The children learn their own limitations. The structures are multi-purpose and the children use them for different reasons. Recently I felt that they were not making good enough use of the space. Markings can help create a wider range of games. The current markings were rather worn and the children did not really use them very much. I want to encourage the children to use the space better, more fully, more effectively. There is a need for new markings to create other play activities and learning opportunities.

I tried to make the children think where to put their games. They need to relate to each other. You have to create safe spaces to play, for movement within and through the space. Safety considerations are very important —the new markings should not be too near structures or in the football area. Structures should not be part of the game, nor should markings be near doors. I explained the need for games to quieten down the rough child and to encourage the timid child. I suggested they should have no definite finishing point so that the game does not end. I thought the children's work was brilliant. The games they suggested were flexible and could be adapted for different children's needs. Their ideas were realistic.

When my three children attended this school, they had nothing to play with. The structures, the planting and the markings have improved the environmental quality. It now looks as if we are caring, that we want to give something to children. It makes the school environment more enjoyable. Playground markings are joyful. They also create more educational opportunities. Play is an important learning activity. If it is enjoyable, children will learn better. It has become a tradition in this school to involve children in making their environment. Children's ideas about play activity are very different from those of adults. I think we should remember this when we are creating play environments.

The Headteacher's view

☐ The Headteacher's Role

I identified the problems, the issues, the difficulties for the teacher, brought people together, sat in on initial meetings, then stepped back. They developed the work. I was kept informed. My current involvement is to provide encouragement and reminders, to ensure that the work is completed. I have commissioned, arranged for payment and will ensure the implementation of the work. I have found the money for an evaluation.

☐ Collaborative Working

I think it is very desirable that teachers work with people from outside. But the relationship needs guidance. The purposes have to be very clear and educational considerations paramount. When I have observed an 'expert' working with children, usually the children's response is better. This is not to devalue the teacher's work. The teacher's expertise as an educator can be enhanced and extended through collaborative working. Some teachers may be very aware of techniques and feel confident and competent. Others would benefit from the support an outside expert can give. Some teachers may not have the skill in using the techniques involved in particular areas of work. The important message to children must be that they can develop these skills through practice.

☐ Environmental Education

We have no written policy on environmental education. The playground is an important focus for caring for the environment — it is pertinent to begin with our own environment. We have attempted to green the playground. The children care for plants. They respect other children's work. They are encouraged to keep their environment clean and tidy. There is a big commitment to experiential learning. We try to create opportunities when it is appropriate.

☐ Environmental Change

Environmental change impinges on the real world. We have a tradition in this school of publishing children's work. When the work becomes public, the purpose of the writing has a real dimension, their ideas are something to be shared. The consequences of this are big — motivation, commitment and quality of work improves. It is about children's autonomy and empowerment, their ability to make democratic decisions.

In future, projects such as the playground project will be funded out of INSET and the building maintenance and development budget. Maintenance of the playground will cost schools money, though I understand that the authority will continue to be responsible for major structural elements. I suspect that the school will have responsibility for safety. The better the environment, the better people feel in it. Then there are aesthetic considerations. Bleak concrete and brick walls do not make an attractive place. That is an unattractive environment for children to be in. How a place looks and feels is important. There are spin-offs in that the playground benefits in terms of aesthetic quality, in the introduction of colour to the environment, in the variety of play options for the children, of choices of what to do.

☐ Play

By improving opportunities for play, we are trying to help people respond positively to the environment they are in. I do not know what research there has been on play in school grounds, but any social interaction can be educational. I am not prepared to quantify the benefits. Playground play is an important component of a child's education. In the playground, children play together, argue, try to resolve conflicts. We will improve the quality of play — and therefore of educational experience — by extending possibilities for social interaction. With better facilities, there are more opportunities for games which enhance experience. We need to develop skills in sharing, co-operation, waiting one's turn. There needs to be a variety of play experience, both physical and social, and a greater range of activities. This will result in children developing greater capabilities. Play which is

restricted to charging around and letting off steam can be inconsiderate and has limited educational value. Play needs to be focused and purposeful. There is an important hidden curriculum here. Play needs to be constructive.

With specific regard to markings, there are three kinds: those for organised games such as netball; those that are for well-established traditional games like hopscotch, the spiral with numbers or ladders — but these are too prescriptive in terms of the range of activities they encourage; then there are the markings that the children create themselves. They design what they want, what they feel would be useful or appropriate. They reflect the games they want to play, to work out themselves and provide for more imaginative use.

Outcomes

☐ Aims

The project must be counted a success if it is evaluated against the original aims, that is:

- to stimulate an interest in numbers, signs and language;

- to develop awareness and knowledge of the environment;

- to encourage co-operation, self-esteem and group pride; and

- to develop an appreciation of the design process.

The variety of learning activities gave the children experience of working with numbers, and of spoken and written language and visual language using plans, diagrams and pictures. They had opportunities to explore different ways of understanding, developing and communicating ideas. In many cases, the same information needed to be expressed in different ways, so that the pupils could begin to identify which language form to use for a particular purpose. Specific objectives requiring the children to be able to read a plan, make bar charts, interview and co-operate as a member of a group were fully addressed.

The use of the immediate environment was challenging, as children tend to take their everyday, familiar surroundings for granted and find it difficult to perceive it anew. However, the project gave them a fresh awareness of their school environment, helped them to understand it more fully and enabled them to consider how they might improve it. The opportunities to compare it with a similar environment helped to develop discriminatory and critical skills.

The children were made more conscious of being members of a class group through various learning activities which involved group working. They learned strategies to cope with these. They were able to compare the value of working independently or within a group. They were proud of their own work and other children's. Although boys will still not voluntarily work with girls, they learnt skills of co-operation and social interaction through group work, and girls now have an enhanced status within the class because of their particular success in the design work. However, the teacher feels that the project did not address multicultural issues.

☐ National Curriculum

As far as the National Curriculum is concerned, it is evident that the work satisfies many of the attainment targets in English, Mathematics and Design and Technology and to a lesser extent in Geography. The cross-curricular themes of Environmental Education and Personal and Social Development are also addressed. Throughout the project, two ideas were of particular importance: Design as a cross-curricular study; and the notion of learning with a purpose.

English

The work involved the pupils in listening, writing and talking activities in a variety of situations which included individual work, group work and class work.

There was an emphasis on spoken language, through which the pupils encountered the excitement of brainstorming, where ideas were generated within a group as well as the challenge of describing a game they had devised. The opportunity to explain a complex set of rules and try to persuade colleagues to accept your idea were all opportunities for the children to develop different language skills. In some cases, this was a prelude to writing. This involved description and explanation about games, a more fantastical piece on their ideal playground and a business letter, when they wrote for advice on costings for the markings to be painted. Listening skills were important in class work and group work. The children were expected to respond to information, advice and direction from both adults and other children.

Mathematics

A large amount of mathematics was involved in preliminary investigations. Measurement of area was carried out and the notion of scale introduced. Tallying and bar charts helped children compare various ways of recording and presenting the same information. Within the design activity, the pupils explored pattern, tessellations and sequences.

Art

In the National Curriculum, Art is seen as a means of observation, research and developing ideas. This was the approach taken in the project, where art activities were an important means for the pupils to visualise possibilities for change, to consider alternatives and to communicate their ideas. They worked from the primary source of the environment itself, from secondary sources of visual reference material and from their imagination.

Design Technology

The project on playground markings emphasised environmental design, but also included the notion of play and games as systems. Some consideration was given to artefacts that can be used in play activities. However, the emphasis throughout the work was on the design process, which addressed both the old and the revised attainment targets.

The project started with an exploration of the idea of play, an evaluation of current play activities in the playground and an identification of the need to extend opportunities for play. The children worked through a process of generating, developing and evaluating their ideas. These were realised and the markings painted. Further evaluation will take place as the children monitor the results of their work.

The project related closely to the attainment targets of designing and making. The pupils investigated, clarified and specified the design task, then modelled, developed and communicated their design ideas and explained how their work might be evaluated. They worked both independently and in groups. The project involved a variety of learning activities. Judgements were made which took account of aesthetic, economic, social and environmental considerations.

Although they did not actually paint the markings on the playground themselves, their design ideas were clearly communicated so that they could be interpreted and carried out by others. This is probably closer to the experience of the world outside school, where designers are not usually responsible for the manufacturing or production process, which is handled by technicians or operatives. This was the case here, where a skilled team of painters were able to put into effect the children's ideas.

When talking about design, the children used words such as *structure, suitable, safety, choice, scale, variety, opportunities, problems* and *cost*. When talking about the design process, they talked about *ideas, thinking out loud, explaining, starting point, drawing, designing, planning ahead* and *choosing*. When discussing the merits of group working, they used expressions such as *teamwork, working together, joining in, taking turns, helping, sharing* and *encouragement*. They were aware of the various phases necessary in developing a design. They described their experience of having a *starting point, generating ideas, selecting* and *developing further, testing it out* and *revising it*. The work has shown the children that they are capable of designing.

Plan-making was an important part of the initial investigations and the design activity but had its limitations. Plans deal with spatial relationships in two dimensions. To understand the impact of the markings on the playground space, it would have been helpful to work in three dimensions or to create a full-scale mock-up, preferably in chalk on the playground. This would have given the pupils a better opportunity to test out their designs.

Environmental Education.

The project provided experience of work in, about and for the environment. It was based on direct experience of the environment, but also made use of secondary sources of information and stimulus, such as books, pictures and games. It is not always possible to ensure that children's work will result in positive action upon the environment, but in this case the opportunity was there and the school chose to take it. The project used the children's new awareness to consider the need for change and to explore possibilities for dealing with this positively and creatively. So often in schools, the environment is presented in negative terms, as a collection of problems to be solved. In this project, the environment was considered as something to be cherished and celebrated. The tangible outcome of the playground markings attest to the success of the work and show it to have a real purpose.

☐ Inter-professional Collaboration

The school would clearly have found it difficult to undertake such a project without the encouragement and support of an outside agency. ISEP's reputation, experience and proven track record in working with schools gave them the confidence to tackle such an ambitious project. The advice and support provided by ISEP created a secure framework for the teacher and pupils to develop their work. The contribution of the play supervisor was important, drawing on a different source of experience and expertise. The working contact with the White Lion Centre provided for a depth of study not always possible in school. For the children, the experience of working with adults other than teachers lent an impetus and excitement to the work which increased their motivation and improved the quality of their work.

For David Stone of ISEP, the project offered a rather different experience from that of previous work. Here, the teacher was an equal partner. The work had to relate to the requirements of the National Curriculum. ISEP did not have control over the implementation, so the designs had to be clear enough for another agency to take over the painting. This meant a greater emphasis on the educational value of the work, but placed David Stone in the dual role of teacher and chief designer, to ensure that the children's ideas could be translated into actual markings on the playground. ISEP is now beginning to work with schools in a different role, that of adviser and catalyst, concentrating more on the educational aspects of the work. The project has provided valuable experience of how such work can fit into the National Curriculum and has demonstrated the kind of work which may be expected of nine year olds.

☐ Professional Development

It is clear that the teacher would have found it more difficult to have developed such a project alone. Although many of the learning activities might be part of the children's normal programme, they would not necessarily have developed into a design project. The experience of working with an artist/designer has changed the teacher's view of design in the curriculum and given her greater confidence to tackle similar projects in future. The production of a slide programme, exhibition and report for other teachers in the school will enable them to learn from their colleague's experience and perhaps reconsider the possibility of environmental design within the Technology curriculum. Making this material more widely available will extend this opportunity to other teachers.

☐ Summary

The playground markings project at Gillespie School realised its aims to engage pupils in collaborative working, to develop their awareness and understanding of design and the environment and to extend their skills in a number of subject areas. The working partnership between the class teacher and the director of the Islington Schools Environmental Project created opportunities for work that would not have been possible otherwise. The project not only satisfied the requirements of the National Curriculum but resulted also in immediate and tangible outcomes of improved play opportunities. The interest and excitement generated by this project will act as stimulus and encouragement for other teachers contemplating similar work.

Questions arising

☐ Design

- How is a need or opportunity for change to be identified?
- What techniques are needed for analysis and appraisal?
- What constitutes environmental improvement? Who decides? How?
- What experience of designers' work can schools provide?
- How far can pupils be involved in the design process?
- What criteria enable pupils to form balanced judgements which take account of functional, aesthetic, economic, social and environmental considerations?
- What are the implications of raising pupils' expectations about change?
- How are children enabled to deal with the practical and financial constraints?

☐ National Curriculum

- Does the school have a policy for Design and Technology across the curriculum?
- What range of work will include a study of artefacts, systems and environments?
- What environmental design projects can incorporate both attainment targets of designing and making?
- What environmental design studies are appropriate for different age groups? How is it possible develop a sense of progression through the different years?
- What are the resource implications for Design and Technology?

☐ Professional and Curriculum Development

- How can the knowledge gained from projects be reinvested in future work?
- How can work be documented and disseminated? How can the pupils contribute?
- How might the work in progress be recorded?
- What simple process of self-evaluation can be adopted?
- How can the results of projects be shared throughout the school?
- How can other teachers benefit?
- How can other pupils benefit?

☐ Roles

- How do the roles of teacher and outsider differ?
- How can the headteacher facilitate the project?
- How might funding be secured?

☐ Environmental Improvement

- How far can pupils be involved in implementation of their proposals?
- How can all members of the school community participate in the design process?
- What are the financial implications of environmental improvements under LMS?
- What are the maintenance implications?

Advice to other schools

☐ Curriculum Development

Schools have to develop their own projects, appropriate to their particular situations. *'I would say go for it. You need to have a particular philosophy or vision, a particular view of learning. It depends on the style and approach of the head-teachers, whether they choose to direct or encourage, whether as a facilitator they can step back and keep a loose rein on the work. Headteachers need to seek opportunities to develop the work of the school in whichever ways they think appropriate.'* Jake Herbst, Headteacher.

'The work needs to be well organised, with clear aims. There is a need to anticipate the total development beforehand, though I do not think you should have a predetermined idea of the work the children will produce. I would advise other teachers not to panic and to be flexible. Do not be afraid to work with others, to accept advice and criticism. And do not be afraid to speak up if things are wrong'. Janet Eccles, Teacher.

☐ Design

Engaging in design requires a positive and optimistic stance, a preparedness to take risks and deal with the unknown. Sometimes this is in conflict with our educational aims, where we want to ensure successful results. If you know the outcome in advance, it defeats the purpose of the design activity. Design always happens within a range of opportunities and constraints. These should be recognised from the outset. *'It is necessary to acknowledge the constraints on the work right from the beginning — timing and weather, for instance. There should be sufficient time for the design work. There is the danger that you spend too much time collecting information and concentrating on initial ideas, that you do not really develop the designs sufficiently. Visualisation is something quite complex. We need to find ways of developing rather than inhibiting it, of testing out and revising our ideas'.* David Stone, ISEP.

☐ Environmental Improvement

The pupils have the last word! *'You need time to develop ideas to improve the playground. The markings are a good idea to make the school beautiful and the environment more interesting for kids. It will be more exciting and help children think better. It is not fair that other schools do not have good things'.*